William Thomas

The ultimate step by step secret to stop smoking NOW!!

Copyright © 2023 by William Thomas

All Rights Reserved. No part of this book may be used or reproduced by any means, graphic, electronic, or mechanical, including photocopying, recording, taping, or by any information storage retrieval system without the written permission of the publisher except in the case of brief quotations embodied in critical articles and reviews.

Introduction

The Simple medication free way to deal with stopping smoking. Figure out how to quit smoking without resolve and converse all wellbeing dangers and secondary effects utilizing Thomas' simple aide. You needn't bother with drug and there is no requirement for nicotine substitution treatment. All that you want to beat desires and triggers is in this basic aide. Peaceful and simple to follow. You can't utilize this regular aide without stopping smoking totally.

❖ Attempt Nicotine Substitution

- ❖ It merits recalling that you're not dependent on smoking, in essence. You're dependent on the nicotine that gives those charming liberating sensation in distressing circumstances.
- ❖ The outcome? Tracking down elective ways of getting a nicotine hit will make it a lot more straightforward to fight the temptation to light a cigarette.
- ❖ Think about addressing your GP regarding nicotine substitution treatment. From solution nasal showers to nicotine inhalers, there are different choices to attempt. Over-the-counter arrangements, (for example, nicotine fixes or gum) could likewise work.

❖

❖ Keep away from Risk Zones

❖ At the point when you first quit smoking, your brain will search for any reason to illuminate. That is the reason it's vital to distinguish and stay away from circumstances (like the bar or while drinking your morning espresso) where you're acclimated with smoking!

❖

❖ Concentrate on Tracks down High Predominance of Smoking Among A medical procedure Patients

❖ By deliberately avoiding these circumstances as well as having an arrangement set up to do things any other way, you can prevent likely triggers from causing a backslide. Engage companions at home, hold a pen to possess your fingers, etc.

❖

❖ Occupy Yourself

- ❖ Interruptions are a priceless transient answer for opposing the desires that make certain to happen. By finding another thing to zero in on, you take your psyche off the drive to smoke! It's basic however viable.

- ❖ How you occupy yourself depends on you, yet one broadly suggested choice is work out. Whether you take a walk, do some push-ups, or run up the steps, it tends to be a magnificent interruption with added actual medical advantages. Bombing that, have a go at writing in a diary, doing a few tasks, or playing with the canine anything that takes your psyche off the cigarettes!

❖

❖ Try different things with Self-Entrancing

❖ Self-spellbinding is one more attempted and-tried strategy for stopping smoking rapidly. By entering a self-incited entrancing state, you become more managable to change, persuaded, and engaged. Surrendering the propensity becomes more straightforward all the while.

❖ Just sit back and relax, the truth of spellbinding isn't similar to what you find in the motion pictures! It isn't wizardry. You're just in a condition of profound unwinding as a rule accomplished through representation and breathing activities.

- When you're in this serene, centered state, you pay attention to as well as rehash to yourself applicable expressions and attestations on smoking end. This sound spellbinding serves to reinvent your psyche mind and, in a little while, you wind up thinking, feeling, and behaving like a non-smoker.

❖ Keep a hankering diary

- A desire diary can assist you with focusing in on your examples and triggers. For a week or so paving the way to your quit date, keep a log of your smoking. Note the minutes in every day when you long for a cigarette:

- What time was it?
- How extraordinary was the desire (on a size of 1-10)?
- What's happening with you?
- Who were you with?
- How were you feeling?
- How could you feel subsequent to smoking?

❖

❖ Occupy yourself.

❖ Do the dishes, turn on the television, clean up, or call a companion. The action doesn't make any difference pretty much lengthy your brain off smoking.

❖

❖ Remind yourself why you quit.

❖ Center around your explanations behind stopping, including the medical advantages (bringing down your gamble for coronary illness and cellular breakdown in the lungs, for instance), further developed appearance, cash you're saving, and improved confidence.

❖

❖ Escape what is happening.

❖ Where you or you're doing might be setting off the hankering. Provided that this is true, a difference in landscape can have a significant effect.

❖ Reward yourself.

❖ Support your triumphs. Whenever you win over a desire, give yourself a prize to keep yourself inspired.

❖Needle therapy

❖ Quite possibly of the most seasoned known clinical strategy, needle therapy is accepted to work by setting off the arrival of endorphins (regular pain killers) that permit the body to unwind. As a smoking suspension help, needle therapy can be useful in overseeing smoking withdrawal side effects.

❖

❖ Conduct Treatment

❖ Nicotine enslavement is connected with the ongoing ways of behaving or customs engaged with smoking. Conduct treatment centers around acquiring new adapting abilities and bringing an end to those propensities.

❖

❖Persuasive Treatments

❖ Self improvement guides and sites can give various ways of propelling yourself to quit any pretense of smoking. One notable model is working out the money related investment funds. Certain individuals have had the option to track down the inspiration to stop by simply working out how much cash they will save. It could be sufficient to pay for a mid year excursion.

❖

❖ Center around your inspirations.

❖ Inspiration fluctuates and this is 100% typical — how might you expand your inspiration when you feel crushed or low?

❖

❖Construct certainty.

❖ Certainty that your endeavor will find true success is significant! How might you build your certainty levels? Your certainty can increment when you make and accomplish a progression of little objectives, when you picture your prosperity and when you feel like you have the instruments prepared for any circumstance.

❖

❖ Stress the executives is critical.

❖ Numerous smokers smoke to oversee pressure, misery, and gloomy feelings. Being ready with alternate ways of dealing with these sentiments can be troublesome and takes a ton of training. What do your non-smoking companions do to oversee pressure?

❖

❖ It's never past the time to stop.

- ❖ While it's ideal to stop smoking as soon as could be expected, stopping smoking at whatever stage in life will upgrade the length and nature of your life. You'll likewise set aside cash and keep away from the issue of going external neglected to smoke. You could actually rouse everyone around you to stop smoking!

❖

❖Gain from previous encounters.

❖ A great many people who smoke have attempted to stop previously and once in a while they get beat pondering past endeavors down. Be that as it may, these encounters instruct us a ton about and what to avoid sometime later! These encounters are steps making a course for future achievement. Ponder what worked for you last time, what didn't work and what you could do any other way this time.

❖

❖You don't need to stop alone.

❖ Telling loved ones that you're attempting to stop and enrolling their help will assist with facilitating the cycle. Master help is accessible from the American Lung Affiliation and different gatherings. Companions who likewise smoke might try and go along with you in attempting to stop!

❖ Drugs are protected and compelling and will help you quit and remain quit when utilized appropriately.

- ❖ Ask your medical services supplier for suggestions. The meds assist with withdrawal side effects, inclinations and desires, yet don't assist with the propensity or with overseeing pressure or pessimistic feelings. Many individuals don't utilize the meds accurately or don't utilize them adequately long or anticipate that the medicine should supplant all that smoking used to accomplish for us. Make certain to follow the bearings and join prescriptions with different instruments for stopping.
- ❖ Each smoker can stop. At the American Lung Affiliation, we immovably accept that each smoker can stop. Everybody is unique and each quit endeavor is somewhat unique. Track down the right blend of apparatuses, prescriptions, and backing for you! Or more all, continue on.

❖

❖It Requires Investment

- ❖ The initial seven to 10 days are the hardest, and you might require the most assistance during these early days. Most smokers who return to smoking do as such inside the initial three months. "Slips" (having a puff, or smoking a couple of cigarettes) are normal. Assuming you've slipped, help yourself to remember every one of the valid justifications to remain quit. A slip doesn't mean you are a smoker once more. As lengthy you continue on and don't surrender, you will actually want to stop for good.

- ❖ Previous smokers at times get inclinations to smoke months or even a very long time after they quit. This is typical. These urges will happen less frequently over the long haul and they'll ultimately stop totally.

❖Stress The board

- Get a lot of rest and practice good eating habits. Absence of rest and over the top sugar are known triggers.
- Use substitutes for oral desires like gum, crude vegetables, carrot sticks, hard sweets, espresso stirrers, straws.
- Stress is a major trigger for smoking.
- Loosen up by taking a couple of slow, full breaths. Breathe in through your nose and breathe out through your mouth. Rehash it multiple times and perceive how you feel.

❖

❖Upkeep

- ❖ At the point when you have desires, consider areas of strength for how have been up until this point.
- ❖ Recall your explanations behind stopping.
- ❖ Decline to allow your dependence on win.
- ❖ Consider the advantages to your wellbeing, funds, and family.
- ❖ Advise yourself that only one cigarette can't really exist.
- ❖ Begin to consider yourself to be a non-smoker. That is a definitive result. You are liberating yourself from the control of your compulsion.

❖ Additional tips

- **View as an oral substitute** - Keep different things around to pop in your mouth when desires hit. Attempt mints, carrot or celery sticks, gum, or sunflower seeds. Or on the other hand suck on a drinking straw.

- **Keep your psyche occupied** - Read a book or magazine, stand by listening to some music you love, do a crossword or Sudoku puzzle, or play a web based game.

- **Keep your hands occupied** - Crush balls, pencils, or paper cuts are great substitutes to fulfill that requirement for material feeling.

- **Clean your teeth** - The fair cleaned, clean inclination can assist with banishing cigarette desires.

- **Hydrate** - Gradually drink an enormous glass of water. Not exclusively will it assist the desire with passing, yet remaining hydrated limits the side effects of nicotine withdrawal.

- **Light something different** - Rather than lighting a cigarette, light a candle or some incense.

- **Get dynamic** - Take a walk, do some hopping jacks or pushups, attempt some yoga stretches, or go around the block.

- **Attempt to unwind** - Accomplish something that quiets you down, like cleaning up, thinking, perusing a book, or rehearsing profound breathing activities.
- **Head off to some place smoking isn't allowed** - Step into a public structure, store, shopping center, bistro, or cinema, for instance.

❖

www.ingramcontent.com/pod-product-compliance
Lightning Source LLC
LaVergne TN
LVHW052114160826
845678LV00015B/3553